50–100 TRILLION

the number of cells in an adult's body

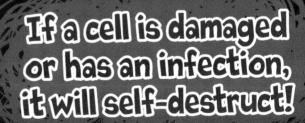

If a cell is damaged or has an infection, it will self-destruct!

MUSCLE CELLS LIVE AS LONG AS YOU DO.

4

Skin cells live for up to 30 days.

WHITE BLOOD CELLS LIVE FOR LESS THAN ONE DAY!

Skin is your body's LARGEST ORGAN.

WITHOUT SKIN YOU WOULD EVAPORATE.

18 KILOGRAMS
(40 POUNDS): THE AMOUNT OF SKIN YOU WILL SHED IN YOUR LIFETIME

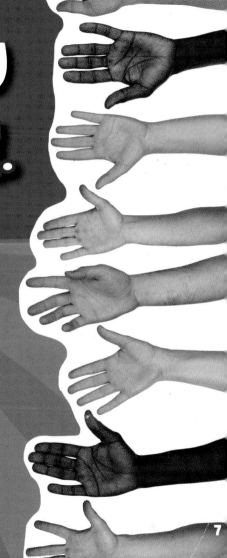

MUSCLES IN THE HUMAN BODY: 639

You use 200 muscles to take one step!

MUSCLES MAKE UP HALF OF YOUR WEIGHT.

To kiss, a person uses 34 FACIAL MUSCLES.

You have 206 bones in your body – 106 of them are in your hands and feet.

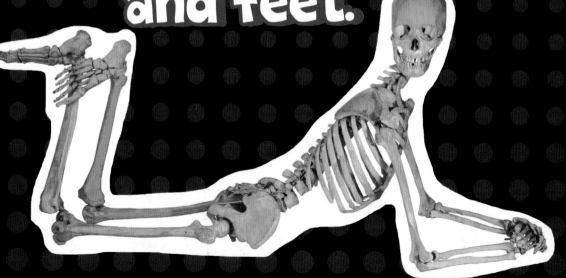

YOUR FEMUR (THIGH BONE) IS THE **STRONGEST** BONE IN YOUR BODY

Some bones are stronger than concrete!

THE AVERAGE NUMBER OF BROKEN
BONES A PERSON WILL HAVE
IN A LIFETIME IS TWO.

Do you want to keep
your bones strong?
Drink more MILK!

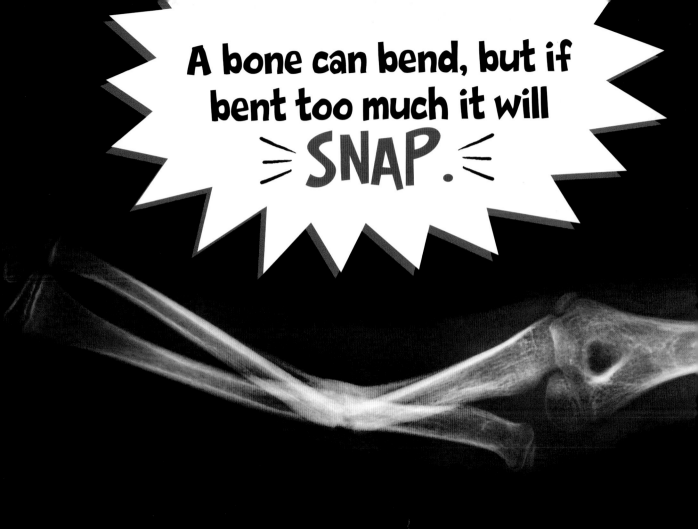

Your teeth are the only bones that can't repair themselves.

Your milk teeth grew before you were born – they were just hiding beneath your gums.

14

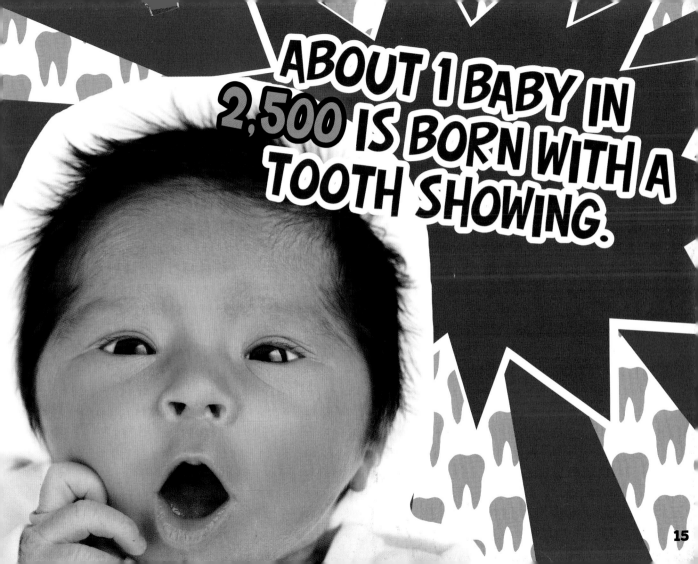

ABOUT 1 BABY IN 2,500 IS BORN WITH A TOOTH SHOWING.

15

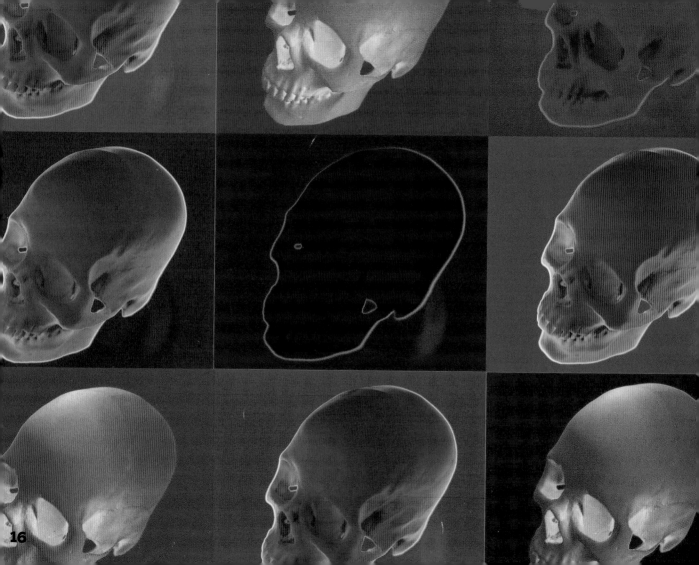

16

AN ADULT'S SKULL IS MADE UP OF 22 BONES.

Your brain is active while YOU SLEEP.

About **80%** of your brain is **WATER.**

THE BRAIN CANNOT FEEL PAIN.

THE NERVOUS SYSTEM IS LIKE THE HUMAN BODY'S ELECTRICAL WIRING.

Neurons send signals through the nervous system. These signals travel at around 100 metres (328 feet) per second!

Your brain has about 100 billion neurons in it!

EYE **LENS** A human has a **LENS** that works very much like a **CAMERA LENS.**

Your **EYES** are made up mostly of a jelly-like goo.

YOU BLINK ABOUT 6,205,000 TIMES IN A YEAR!

23

SOME PEOPLE CAN HEAR THEIR EYEBALLS MOVING.

EXOPHTHALMOS

IS A CONDITION IN WHICH A PERSON'S EYEBALLS BULGE.

SOME PEOPLE ARE BORN WITHOUT IRISES – THE **COLOURED PARTS** OF THE EYES.

ALMOST ALL ADULTS HAVE **MITES** LIVING ON THEIR EYELASHES.

MITES

Some people have
two rows of
EYELASHES.

YOUR THUMB IS THE SAME LLENGTH AS YOUR NOSE.

Your ears and nose never stop growing.

YOUR NOSE CONTAINS CARTILAGE - THE SAME SUBSTANCE THAT MAKES UP A SHARK'S SKELETON.

Some people snore louder than the sound of a **PNEUMATIC DRILL** on cement!

60% OF MEN OVER THE AGE OF 60 SNORE.

ZZZZZZ

33

Less than 2 per cent of people in the world have red hair.

YOUR HAIR IS DEAD. THAT'S WHY IT DOESN'T HURT WHEN YOU GET A HAIRCUT.

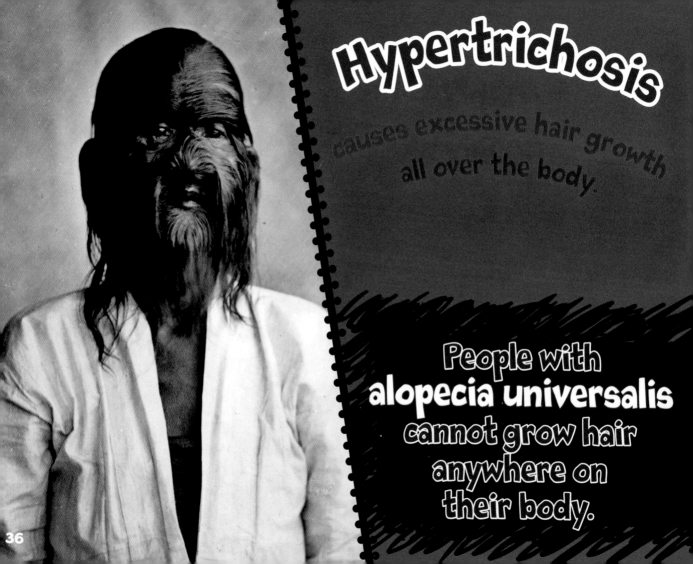

Hypertrichosis

causes excessive hair growth all over the body.

People with **alopecia universalis** cannot grow hair anywhere on their body.

BLONDES HAVE MORE HAIR THAN PEOPLE WITH OTHER HAIR COLOURS.

EVERY DAY YOU LOSE ABOUT 75 STRANDS OF HAIR.

LIPS DO NOT SWEAT.

YOUR LIPS GET THINNER AS YOU GET OLDER.

Very thin skin covers lips. The blood underneath the skin makes lips look red!

39

YOUR TONGUE IS ONE OF THE **STRONGEST MUSCLES** IN YOUR BODY.

The longest human tongue ever recorded was 10 centimetres (4 inches) long!

EVERY TONGUE PRINT IS UNIQUE.

No one is exactly sure why we yawn.

People yawn more during the winter.

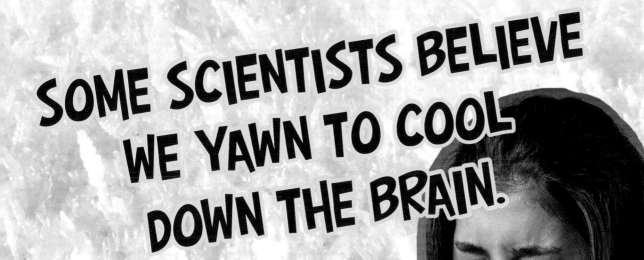

SOME SCIENTISTS BELIEVE WE YAWN TO COOL DOWN THE BRAIN.

Most yawns last about 6 seconds.

43

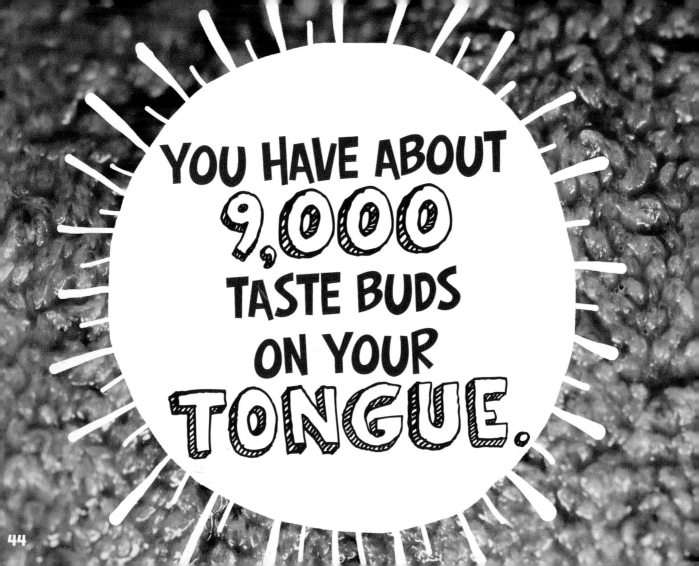

YOU HAVE ABOUT 9,000 TASTE BUDS ON YOUR TONGUE.

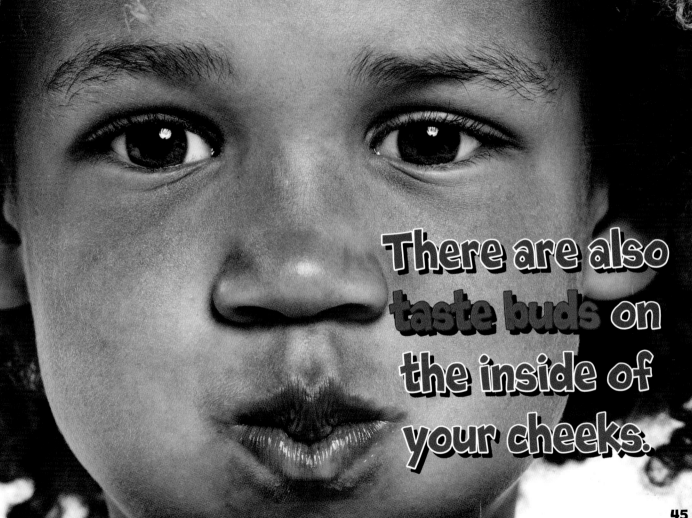

There are also taste buds on the inside of your cheeks.

45

A sneeze can travel at up to 160 kilometres (100 miles) per hour.

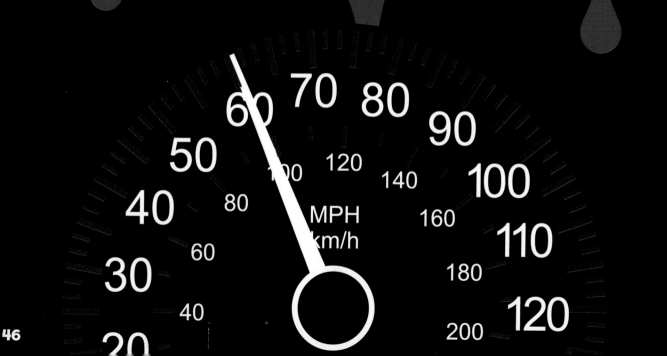

Donna Griffiths, a 12-YEAR-OLD from England, sneezed for 978 days in a row!

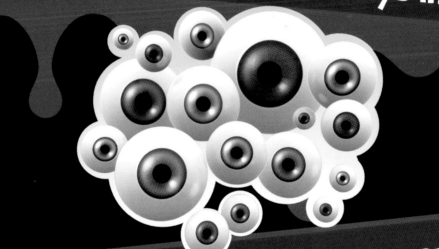

It is impossible to keep your eyes open when you sneeze.

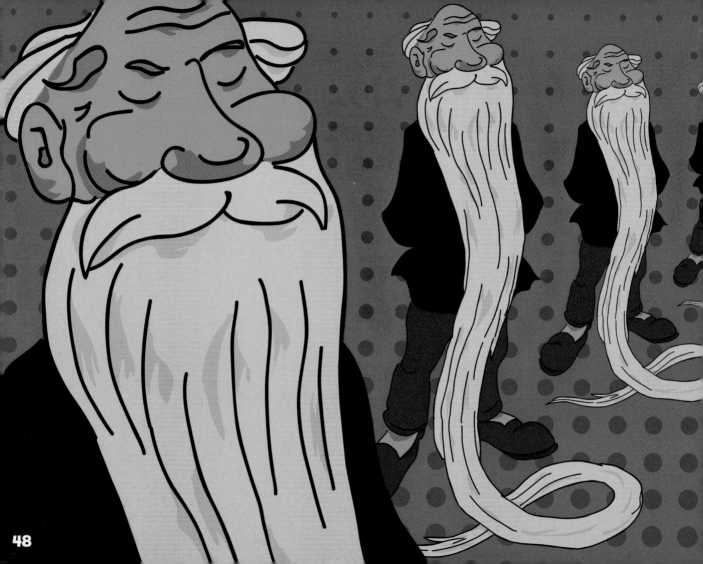

IF A MAN NEVER CUT HIS BEARD, IT COULD GROW TO BE 9 METRES (30 FEET) LONG IN HIS LIFETIME.

49

WHEN YOU'RE SCARED, YOUR EARS MAKE EXTRA EARWAX.

50

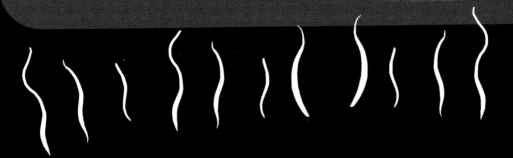

Earwax is not really wax. It's a mixture of oil, sweat, hair and dead skin.

IN THE PAST, EARWAX WAS USED AS LIP BALM!

AN AVERAGE HUMAN HEART WILL BEAT ABOUT

2.5 BILLION
TIMES IN A LIFETIME.

A heart can beat outside of a body for a short time.

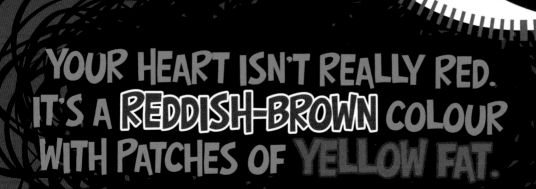

YOUR HEART ISN'T REALLY RED. IT'S A **REDDISH-BROWN** COLOUR WITH PATCHES OF **YELLOW FAT.**

53

YOUR BODY CONTAINS ABOUT 96,500 KILOMETRES (60,000 MILES) OF BLOOD VESSELS!

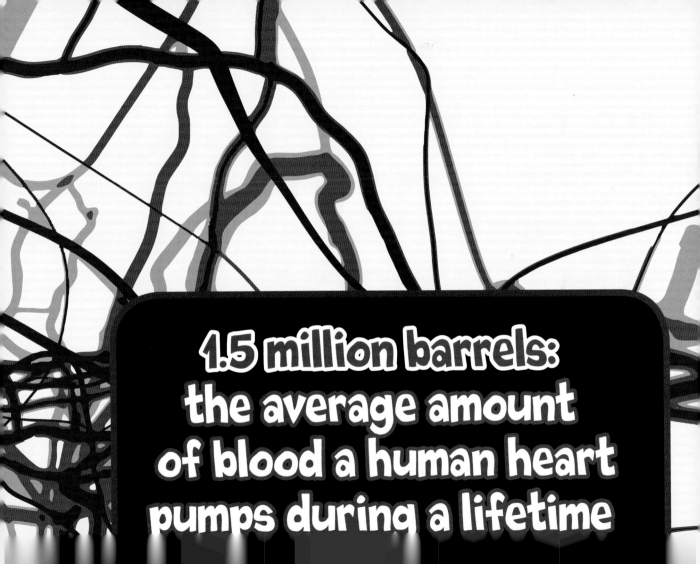

1.5 million barrels:
the average amount
of blood a human heart
pumps during a lifetime

You have about **25 TRILLION** red blood cells.

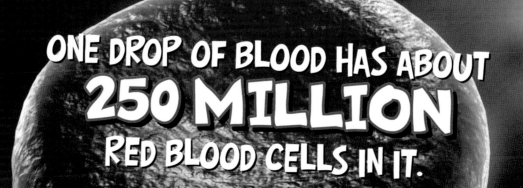

ONE DROP OF BLOOD HAS ABOUT **250 MILLION** RED BLOOD CELLS IN IT.

SOME PEOPLE CAN PLAY THE PIANO WITH THEIR TOES.

More than half of the world's population has one foot that is bigger than the other.

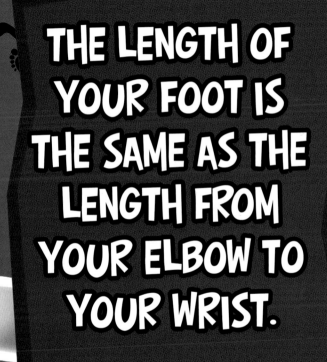

THE LENGTH OF YOUR FOOT IS THE SAME AS THE LENGTH FROM YOUR ELBOW TO YOUR WRIST.

Pig and cow heart valves can be used to replace unhealthy heart valves in humans.

If you lose a finger, a toe can be sewn on to replace it.

Fingernails grow about THREE TO FOUR times faster than toenails.

IF YOU LOSE A TOENAIL, IT MAY TAKE ONE YEAR FOR IT TO GROW BACK.

Nails curl when you let them grow very long.

MILLIONS OF MICROSCOPIC CREATURES LIVE BENEATH YOUR NAILS.

You are tallest in the morning, because gravity pulls down on your body throughout the day.

THE TALLEST PERSON EVER WAS ROBERT WADLOW.
HE MEASURED 2.7 METRES (8 FEET, 11 INCHES) TALL.

ASTRONAUTS

ARE 5 CENTIMETRES (2 INCHES) TALLER WHILE THEY ARE IN SPACE.

LUNGS ARE SPONGY.

The left lung is smaller than the right lung.

The average human takes about 7 million breaths in one year.

YOU HAVE AROUND
1.600 KILOMETRES
(1,000 MILES) OF AIRWAYS
IN YOUR BODY.

Sweat is like air conditioning for your body.

Sweat doesn't have an odour. It's the bacteria that live near the sweat glands that **smell.**

MOST PEOPLE SWEAT

ABOUT 1,000 LITRES (278 GALLONS)

PER YEAR.

THERE ARE 500,000 SWEAT GLANDS
IN YOUR FEET.

STRESSED OUT?

Your body makes a hormone called adrenaline when you're under stress.

Your kidneys look like giant kidney beans. They're about 10 centimetres (4 inches) long, or about the length of your hand.

KIDNEYS FILTER ABOUT 189 LITRES (50 GALLONS) OF BLOOD PER DAY. THAT'S ENOUGH TO FILL A LARGE DUSTBIN!

YOUR SPLEEN IS SOFT AND PURPLE AND IS ABOUT THE SIZE OF YOUR FIST.

YOU CAN LIVE WITHOUT YOUR SPLEEN.

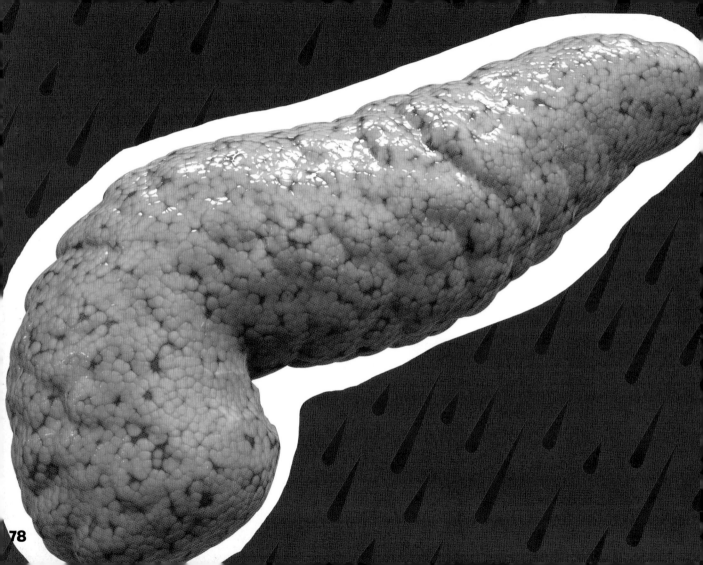

A PANCREAS IS SHAPED A BIT LIKE A SOCK.

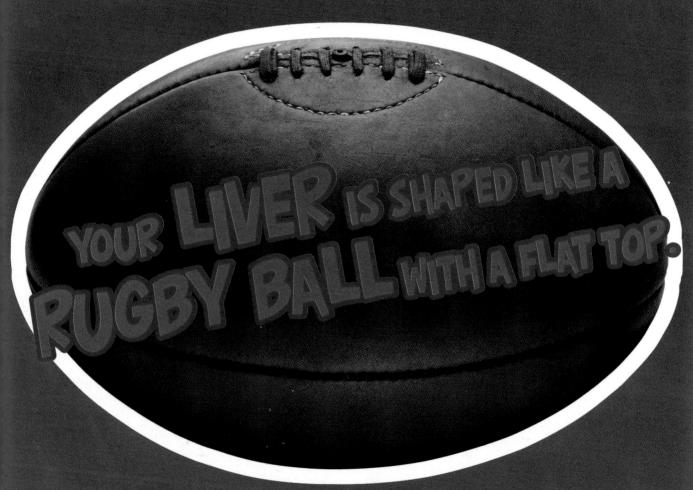

YOUR **LIVER** IS SHAPED LIKE A **RUGBY BALL** WITH A FLAT TOP.

At 1.6 KILOGRAMS (3 ½ pounds), the liver wins the title for the heaviest internal organ.

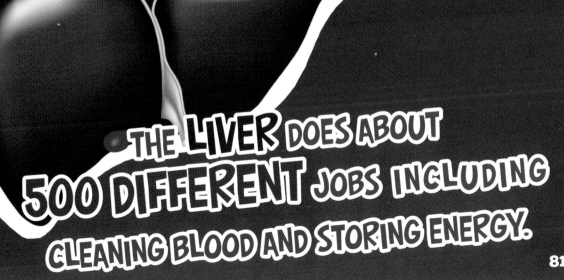

THE **LIVER** DOES ABOUT 500 DIFFERENT JOBS INCLUDING CLEANING BLOOD AND STORING ENERGY.

BILE, A LIQUID MADE BY THE LIVER, IS BRIGHT GREEN.

83

YOUR **BELLY BUTTON** IS REALLY A SCAR WHERE YOUR

UMBILICAL CORD WAS CUT.

84

DO YOU THINK YOU'RE CLEAN?

MANY DIFFERENT BACTERIA LIVE INSIDE YOUR BELLY BUTTON!

YOU CAN LIVE FOR ABOUT ONE WEEK WITHOUT WATER.

A HUMAN CAN LIVE FOR UP TO TWO MONTHS WITHOUT FOOD.

THE FOOD YOU EAT SPENDS ABOUT 2 TO 4 HOURS IN YOUR STOMACH.

Your stomach is full of acid. It's what breaks down your food.

THE ACID IN YOUR STOMACH IS SO STRONG IT CAN DISSOLVE METAL!

89

IF COMPLETELY UNCOILED, YOUR INTESTINES WOULD BE ABOUT 8 METRES (25 FEET) LONG.

THAT'S ABOUT AS LONG AS AN ORCA.

DID YOU KNOW THAT FAECES CAN BE PURPLE OR BLUE?

You will poo about 7 TONNES of faeces in your lifetime.

93

WHEN YOUR BLADDER IS FULL, IT IS THE SIZE OF A GRAPEFRUIT.

95

You may have 6 BILLION bacteria living in your mouth.

Some BACTERIA help you to digest foods. Other bacteria help protect your gums.

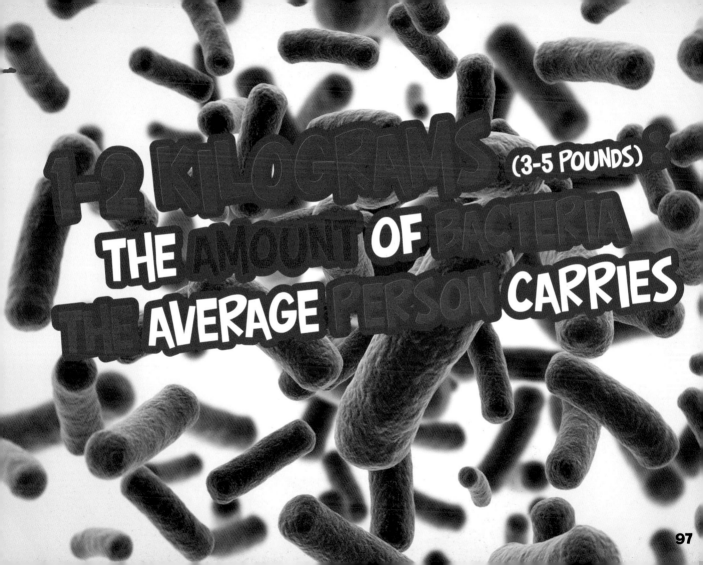

1-2 KILOGRAMS (3-5 POUNDS):
THE AMOUNT OF BACTERIA THE AVERAGE PERSON CARRIES

EVERYBODY FARTS!
SOME PEOPLE JUST DON'T ADMIT IT.

FIZZY DRINKS AND BUBBLEGUM CAN MAKE YOU FART MORE.

Some people eat their HAIR.

THE LARGEST HAIR BALL
REMOVED FROM A PERSON'S STOMACH WEIGHED
4.5 KILOGRAMS
(10 POUNDS)!

YOU PROBABLY HAVE ENOUGH FAT IN YOUR BODY TO MAKE ABOUT 75 CANDLES.

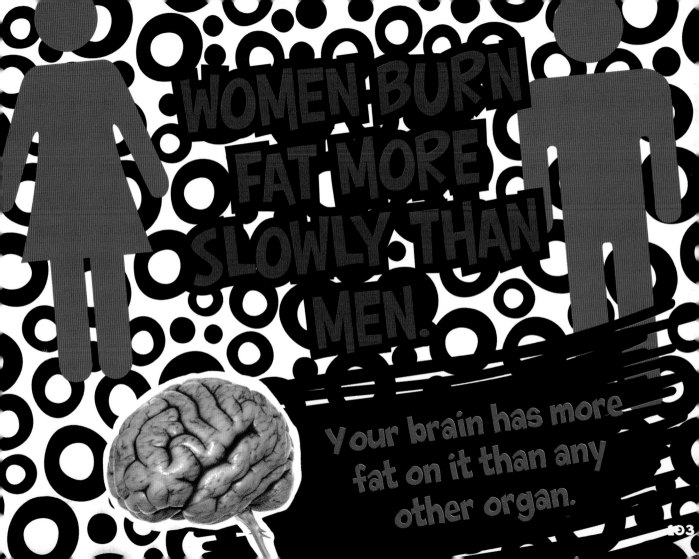

WOMEN BURN FAT MORE SLOWLY THAN MEN.

Your brain has more fat on it than any other organ.

103

YOUR BODY MAKES ABOUT 3 FULL CANS WORTH OF PHLEGM AND MUCUS PER DAY.

104

THE LOUDEST BURP RECORDED WAS 118.1 DECIBELS – ABOUT AS LOUD AS A PLANE TAKING OFF!

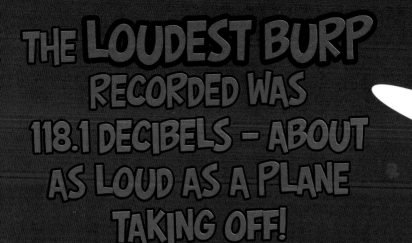

The faster you eat, the more excess air you will have.

HUMANS CAN SEE ABOUT 10 MILLION DIFFERENT COLOURS.

YOU **HEAR** THINGS WHILE YOU SLEEP, BUT YOUR BRAIN DOESN'T DETECT THE SOUNDS.

YOUR NOSE CAN DETECT ABOUT 1 TRILLION DIFFERENT SMELLS.

GLOSSARY

bacteria very small living things that exist all around you and inside you; some bacteria cause disease

bile green liquid made by the liver that helps to digest food

cell basic part of an animal or plant that is so small you can't see it without a microscope

detect notice something; your sense organs detect things about your surroundings

filter remove unwanted materials

gland organ in the body that makes natural chemicals or helps substances to leave the body

heart valve part of the heart that opens and closes to let blood in and out

hormone chemical made by a gland in the body that affects a person's growth and development

liver organ responsible for making bile and storing body oils; the liver cleans blood and helps digestion

neuron nerve cell

oesophagus tube that carries food from the mouth to the stomach; muscles in the oesophagus push food into the stomach

organ part of the body that does a certain job; your heart, lungs and kidneys are organs

pancreas organ near the stomach that makes insulin

spleen organ that is part of the immune system and helps to remove blood cells

umbilical cord tube that connects an unborn baby to its mother

READ MORE

A Day Inside the Human Body (Fantasy Field Trips), Claire Throp (Raintree, 2014)

Utterly Amazing Human Body, Robert Winston (DK Children, 2015)

Why Do I Burp?: Digestion and Diet (Inside My Body), Isabel Thomas (Raintree, 2011)

Your Skin and Bones: Understand them with numbers (Your Body By Numbers), Melanie Waldron (Raintree, 2014)

WEBSITES

www.bbc.co.uk/science/humanbody/body/

Your body is amazing. It is made up of lots of different parts that do different jobs.

www.dkfindout.com/uk/human-body/

Discover more about the amazing human body!

INDEX

Raintree is an imprint of Capstone Global Library Limited, a company incorporated in England and Wales having its registered office at 264 Banbury Road, Oxford, OX2 7DY – Registered company number: 6695582

www.raintree.co.uk
myorders@raintree.co.uk

Text © Capstone Global Library Limited 2016
The moral rights of the proprietor have been asserted.

Editor: Shelly Lyons
Designer: Lori Bye
Media Researcher: Jo Miller

ISBN 978 1 4747 1278 1 (hardback)
20 19 18 17 16
10 9 8 7 6 5 4 3 2 1

ISBN 978 1 4747 1283 5 (paperback)
21 20 19 18 17
10 9 8 7 6 5 4 3 2 1

British Library Cataloguing in Publication Data
A full catalogue record for this book is available from the British Library.

Acknowledgements
We would like to thank the following for permission to reproduce photographs: Alamy: The Natural History Museum, 36; Getty Images: Digital Vision, 16; Newscom: Everett Collection, 66, (right), REX/Philip Reeves, 65; Science Photo Library/Steve Gschmeissner, 26–27; Shutterstock: aarows, 46, Air Images, 45, Aleks Melnik, 79, Aleksandr Bryliaev, 18, Alesikka, 42–43, Alexander Pekour, 95, AlexanderZe, 24, Andrey Armyagov, 25, art_of_sun, 20, ArtHeart, 62, Artishok, 63, Ben Schonewille, 74, bikeriderlondon, 96, Blamb, 94, blambca, 83, (right), block23, 19, Carlos Caetano, 43, chikapylka, 107, Constantine Pankin, 48, Coprid, 104, CREATISTA, 100, Darren Brode, 15, dedek, 91, Designua, 4, Dmitry Kalinovsky, 32, East, 8, Ebic, 67, Eldad Carin, 101, EMcgiq, 103, Gencho Petkov, 84, Gun2becontinued, 55, Haver, 60, HitToon.Com, 86, (right), i3alda, 86, (left), imageerinx, 47, Irina Mir, 92, Jezper, 97, Jiri Miklo, 37, jorgen mcleman, 34, joshya, 5, joshya, 88, JPagetRFPhotos, 50, Juan Gaertner, 90, Kite_rin, 35, Komsan Loonprom, 2, Konstantin Faraktinov, 75, kubais, 12, (bottom), kurhan, 39, leolintang, 64, (top), Liya Graphics, 58–59, , 68, Luis Louro, 72, mart, 108, Matt Antonio, 87, Maya2008, 53, monika3steps, Cover, (bottom left), murat5234, 64, (bottom), n_eri, 102, Nathalie Spellers Ufermann, 44, Oleksii Natykach, 81, Orla, Cover, (top left), Pagina, 54, Palau, 33, PathDoc, 23, , 83, (left), , 93, pedalist, 12, (top), Perfect Vectors, 73, Philipp Nicolai, back cover, 10, photka, 7, Pinon Road, 69, Piotr Marcinski, 61, Puwadol Jaturawutthichai, 13, Radu Bercan, 41, RedKoala, 22, Robert Adrian Hillman, 52, Robin Crossman, 105, Rocketclips, Inc, 14, Sebastian Kaulitzki, 78, Sergey Korkin, 76, SFerdon, 106, solarseven, 30–31, sss615, 85, Stock Up, 80, Suzanne Tucker, 9, , 89, TinnaPong, 109, tommaso lizzul, 28, TsuneoMP, Cover, (top right), VERSUSstudio, Cover, (bottom left), Vinicius Tupinamba, 99, Vira Mylyan-Monastyrska, 66, (left), vitstudio, 21, Volt Collection, 70, whitehoune, 56–57, www.BillionPhotos.com, 38, Yayayoyo, 98, yomogi1, 11, yrchello108, 51.

Design elements by Capstone and Shutterstock.

Printed and bound in China.